EMAIL MARKETING SUCCESS

How to Build an Email List and Create Successful Email Marketing Campaigns

C.X. CRUZ

Table of Contents

Introduction

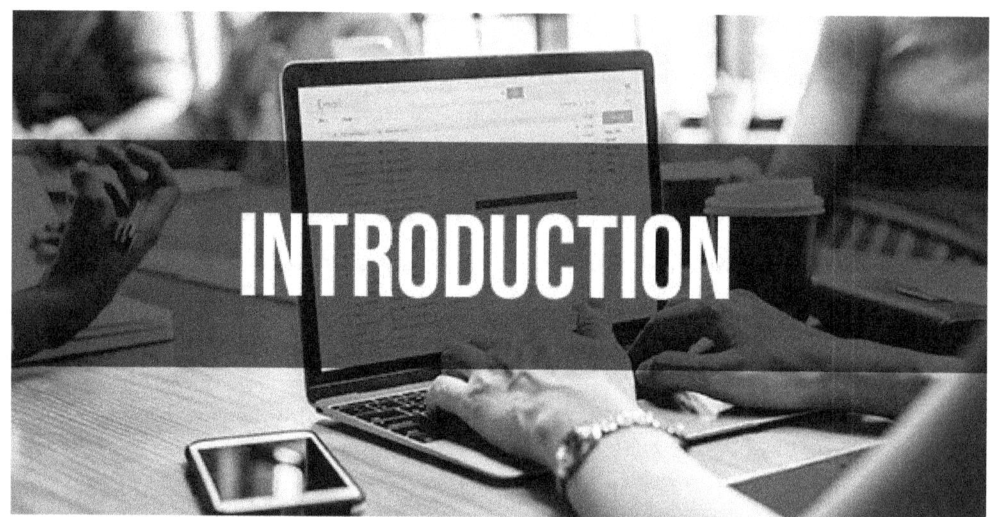

Email marketing for businesses isn't a new concept. In fact, compared to other online marketing channels like social media, mobile device applications, and even search engines, email marketing might seem a bit outdated.

A lot has been happening over the past few years with email marketing, and the discipline is still always in motion. Altered behaviors and expectations by consumers call for new email marketing methods. Approaches like personalization and segmentation are transforming company newsletters from anonymous bulk emails into customized emails.

Today, most consumers read their emails on their mobile devices, and checking for emails has become the most common activity carried out by smartphone users. The competition for attention in consumers email inboxes is forcing more companies to attach increasing importance to well-designed emails which are personalized and have relevant content, ensuring that the emails will be opened and read.

Statistics show that email marketing has a broad reach, as well as being one of the best marketing tactics for return on investment. Just about everyone has an email address these days, and the majority of users prefer to receive advertising messages that way.

Plus, with smartphones, emails are always right in the pocket of consumers and can be retrieved at any time. According to recent estimates, the importance of email marketing will continue to grow over the next few years. It's clear that any online marketing strategy your company employs should include email marketing campaigns.

Email marketing requires more than just sending out the occasional newsletter. Today, marketers also need to set up and maintain subscriber lists, create and design relevant emails, and send these out systematically.

For your email marketing strategy to be effective and successful, it is imperative that you utilize the technical options available continuously optimize the process through the use of modern analytical tools.

Despite the widespread use of the digital juggernaut that is email, many entrepreneurs have yet to implement an effective email marketing strategy for their business because they don't know how to do it or haven't yet recognized how powerful it can be.

Email continues to serve as the core communication platform of the Internet and will only continue to grow. Currently, more than 3.7 billion people have access to email, and more than 3 billion non-spam emails are sent and received every hour of every day.

If your business isn't already taking advantage of this powerful and massive marketing channel, you're missing out on an effective way to reach your target audience.

Chapter 1 – What's Email Marketing and Why Your Business Needs It

Email marketing is a kind of Internet marketing that allows the user to send customized messages in the form of an email to their readers to inform, advertising, or to solicit certain actions from their readers.

There are certain essential components of email marketing that include:

- Message automation
- HTML responsive layout

- Advance list maintenance
- CAN-SPAM compliance built-in

- An easy integration
- A dedicated IP address
- Help for deliverability

Message Automation

The message automation is the feature of email marketing that allows you to send different emails in response to a particular action. If a consumer just signed up for a discount, they will receive an automatic welcome message that will serve as a confirmation of the subscription. Message automation can also be set up to send proof of orders when someone makes a purchase on your website.

HTML Responsive Layout

The HTML Responsive layout will allow you to send customized emails in plain text or HTML format. It also allows you to make use of HTML and CSS to create responsive templates that can adapt to all devices in the world.

This makes email marketing campaigns capable of being read on mobile devices. The good part is that you don't have to learn how to code HTML because this feature is automatically loaded with the software.

Advanced List Maintenance

This feature allows you to add and remove email subscribers from your list quickly. You can use this feature to automate subscription and opt-outs. It helps you keep your email lists updated.

CAN-SPAM Compliance

This is a feature that is designed to check compliance with the unsolicited pornography and marketing, CAN-SPAM Act of 2003. This act has given the United States Federal Trade Commission the right to enforce all necessary standards to protect email owners from unsolicited contents like pornography.

Easy Integration Feature

This feature allows for the integration of other services into your email marketing campaign. You can incorporate your e-commerce website with your email campaigns through this feature, and you can also include several mobile apps, loyalty programs, and social media apps to your email marketing campaign.

You can connect Google analytics to your email campaign through Easy Integration feature so you can track the clicks on your email, as well as incorporating product recommendation features into the email, through the use of this feature.

Dedicated IP Address

A dedicated IP address is incredibly essential for the integrity of your email. This IP address should be one that is solely dedicated to your business, and it should be the only one used to send emails to potential customers. Your email recipients will have peace of mind when they receive your emails with this dedicated IP address.

Deliverability

Deliverability is a feature that is included in an email marketing software that ensures that your emails are delivered to the right place. If your emails aren't delivered, then your marketing strategy just won't work. This features constantly deploys the tools that you need to track down deliverability issues with your emails.

Why Your Business Should Implement Email Marketing

Email provides you with the opportunity to send a message to your audience for any purpose on any day of the year that costs you next to nothing. This makes email an incredibly powerful way to communicate with your target audience.

When you are able to create a solid email marketing campaign and send the right messages to the right people at the right time, you are sure to build an audience of highly engaged fans that can't wait for your next message to hit their inboxes. Additionally, they are ready to buy whenever you have a product or service to promote. There are several compelling reasons why you need to start implementing email marketing for your business.

Generates Massive ROI

A recent study conducted by the Direct Marketing Association found that businesses will earn an average of $43.00 for every dollar invested in email marketing.

In fact, marketers have consistently ranked email marketing as the single most effective strategy for generating awareness, acquiring leads, generating sales, and improving customer retention, compared to the other marketing strategies most commonly employed.

Generates Long-Term Results

In 2010, the company MarketBeat first started collecting opt-ins for their newsletters. Almost two decades later a good number of subscribers that signed up during the first year continue to read their content, engage with their advertisers, and buy products and services from their business.

Your email list is a long-term asset that will continue to generate revenue and social capital for your business well into the future.

Most Customers Want Email from Companies

MarketingSherpa conducted a study that showed that 72 percent of U.S. consumers say that email is their favorite way to communicate with the companies that they do business with. They also discovered that 61 percent of consumers like to receive weekly promotional emails from their favorite brands, while 28 percent of consumers would like to receive promotional emails more frequently.

Additionally, 70 percent of consumers say they will always open email from their favorite companies, and 95 percent of people who opted in to receive an email from brands say that the marketing emails they receive are incredibly useful.

Outperforms Social Media Marketing

A recent study found that businesses are more than 40 times likely to create a new customer from email marketing than they are through social media. When it comes to email marketing, many marketers feel that it delivers a better return on investment than social media marketing.

Email is Universal

Almost 87 percent of the U.S. population has access to the Internet in their home, and 95 percent of consumers use email. With email marketing, you don't have to worry whether or not your target audience has an email address or not, unlike social media.

It's a Resilient Technology

Email has existed in its current format since the early 1980s, a full 15 years before most homes had a personal computer and Internet access, and 25 years before the first iPhone was released. Despite the world's massive amount of technological progress and the proliferation of smartphones, personal computers, and tablets, the technical specifications for email have only been updated a handful of times.

While other communication technologies have come and gone, email continues to withstand the test of time. When your business invests in email marketing, you know that a bigger and better thing won't replace it in the next couple of years.

Email Marketing Is Federated

When you build an audience on YouTube, Facebook or Instagram, you are at the mercy of companies whose best interests aren't aligned with yours.

You can put a lot of time, energy, and money into building an audience on one of these platforms only to have that platform change the rules in a way that kills the profitability of your campaign. That will never be the case with email because no one company has control of the technical specifications for email or control over the technology infrastructure that allows email to be delivered to the world's six billion inboxes.

Email marketing will continue to be one of the most effective and most resilient marketing strategies for both brick-and-mortar companies and digital businesses. It is hard to match the potential ROI offered by email marketing, and you can rest assured that your efforts will continue to generate revenue well into the future.

Chapter 2 – Getting Started with Email Marketing

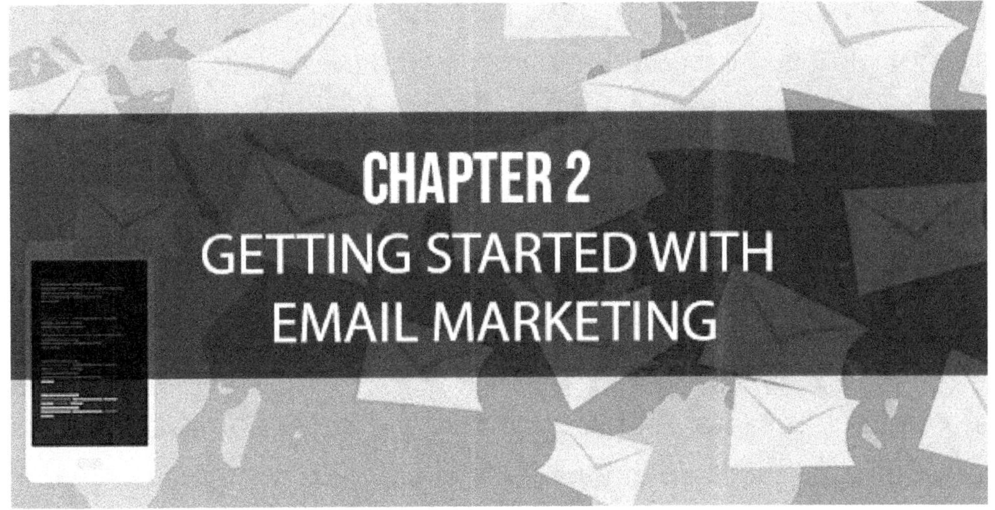

When it comes to starting an email marketing campaign, there are specific steps that you should follow if you want to be successful.

You need to establish clear goals and objectives, build your business email lists, choose the type of email campaign that you want to send, create and design your first email campaign and measure your mail campaign results.

Establishing Your Goals and Objectives

Like with any marketing strategy, you need to develop clear goals and understand your objectives before you dive in head first.

Before you sign up for an email marketing tool, you have to clearly set out what it is you want to achieve with the emails that you want to send to your target audience. You want to make sure that your email marketing campaign aligns with your broader business goals and objectives.

For instance, your business goals might be to attract new leads to sign up for your branded products and services, or perhaps to get more attendees to attend your company events, or maybe you are looking to get more donations for a specific cause. Whatever your overall business goals are, you have to make sure you take the time to think about how you are going to use your email marketing campaign to reach those goals.

Building Your Business Email Lists

After you've established your email marketing campaign goals and objectives, you can start to create your email lists so you can start sending out your email marketing campaigns. There are several ways that you can go about building your email lists. The first option is by importing emails from known contacts.

These are typically the details that you have on your existing customers that you can import into your email marketing tool. You can either manually enter these addresses into your email marketing software, or you can link your email marketing tool to your email account to automatically extract the information.

Another option that you may want to consider is to build an entirely new list of emails from scratch. If you don't have any new contacts currently, you might want to head over to social media to try and entice people from your network to subscribe to your email list by providing them with special discounts or freebies.

You can also utilize your company's website for this as well. You need to make sure that you write compelling content that will get your audience to take action, as well as offering an exclusive first order discount or a freebie for those people who submit their emails from your website or social media network.

Choose the Type of Campaign You Want to Send

You can maximize the effectiveness of your email marketing campaign by following the ten most common and popular formats of emails. These formats have been tested for years and are practiced by top businesses people and established companies.

Each format is unique and has a distinctive purpose, which attracts the interest of different kinds of audiences. Whichever format you choose, each will generate its own kind of reaction.

Newsletters

Newsletters are used for company information, upcoming events, etc. The typical format consists of two columns: one narrow column with a table of contents, logos, sponsors, and feature articles and another wider column with stories and original communication articles and materials.

If there is more than one article, then it's better to use section breaks to make it look smart and eye-catching. You can even put a Read More or Learn More button at the end of each article for detailed information for readers who are interested to know more.

Events and Invitations

This type of email is time sensitive, so you have to be aware of the perfect timing. There should be a buffer of at least a month after an event/invitation email is sent so that your subscribers can decide and make time to prepare.

Every event/invitation email must contain call-to-action buttons, such as a Save to Calendar button, Register for Event button, which will redirect them to another site consisting of forms and

Post-Event Feedback Survey Form button for your company's convenience.

You can also send your audience event details after the event date to all those subscribers who showed interest in the event email, both the attendees and the non-attendees. You may have to send dozens of emails before, during and after the event, so keep your emails short and to the point.

Promotions

This format is used for promotional discounts and special sales of your products and services. You can highlight Limited Edition or Stock Limited products in these emails and get a quick response from your customers. You can also put a call-to-action button like Book Now or Order Now if you are an e-Commerce store.

Setting a deadline on the offer in the email gives the customers that extra push to use the offer right on the spot. Your email marketing campaign will be highly successful if you can make your customers buy products directly from the promotional email.

Press Releases

If you want to share any company information, like the latest business partnerships, new CEO, or new product launches to the local media, then you have to follow the press release format of the email. For this kind of email only, you should make a separate email list where there are just a few addresses for the local media outlets.

Press release emails are different than other formats because others will use it as a reference when they show this information on TV or in the newspaper. Magazines and news portals will write an article based on the information that is contained in your press release, so you need to make sure that it is full of valuable information and that it is share-worthy. There are four sections in a press release: the headline, the body, any statement or quote, and an "about" section.

Announcements

This is similar to a press release, but the audience you will send these emails to is entirely different. Mainly the customers and those who are interested in your company's latest updates are the ones that should get announcement emails.

Announcements could be moving into a new location, product updates, or upcoming product launch information. Only facts and specific information are put in announcements emails, so there is no need for any call-to-action button.

Holiday Greetings

You can design and use special email templates during the holidays, such as one for Halloween, Christmas, or New Year's. Nowadays you can use special HTML or GIF images to make your greeting cards more interesting.

Currently, many ESPs allow you to track customer's birthdays so you can even send them a birthday wish email on their special day. This can help to boost your image and prove that you care about your customers.

Welcome Note

You can set an automated system to send a welcome email to new customers that have recently registered and subscribed to your email service. With a simple "Hello X! Welcome to Y" message you can create a friendly atmosphere with your new customers.

Thank You Email

When you reach a certain level and have hundreds of loyal customers that are buying your products and using your services for years, it's important to show them appreciation. Every year or even twice a year, you should send out thank you emails to your loyal customers.

Most of the time, companies send thank you emails on the day when the company itself was founded. It shows you appreciate your customers and it allows them to feel a deeper connection with your brand.

Notification/Reminder Emails

These kinds of emails remind subscribers about any renewal notifications or service reminder notifications. These kinds of emails typically don't require a call-to-action button to be placed in the body of the email.

Certifications and Confirmation Emails

You would typically only send this type of email for verification of certain agreement forms and certifications, which require step-by step tasks. You must make these steps as easy as possible by including several call-to-action buttons. The "I have read the terms and conditions and agree" type of email falls under this category.

Creating Your First Email Marketing Campaign

The first step that you must take when you create your first email marketing campaign is to structure it for easy reading. With adult attention spans getting shorter and shorter, it is essential that you create emails that are easy for the average adult to get through.

You want to create precise copy for the sole purpose of driving your audience toward the final call-to-action.

Next, you are going to want to customize your email campaign. You can utilize a segmented list or even the third-party integration that comes with most email marketing programs to personalize your campaign.

To encourage more interaction with your campaign customization, you want to make sure that you add the individual name on the subject line to attract the reader's attention, and then create copy that includes relevant information based on their interests.

You want to make sure that you are using all of the data the subscriber provides when the sign up to determine the kind of content you want to send them.

You also need to make sure that your email campaign makes it extremely easy to convert the reader to a new lead or customers. You need to ensure that your email campaign is easy to read since more than 40 percent of readers open their emails on a mobile device. This means it's essential that your email campaign is compatible with mobile devices.

Chapter 3 – Building Your Mailing List

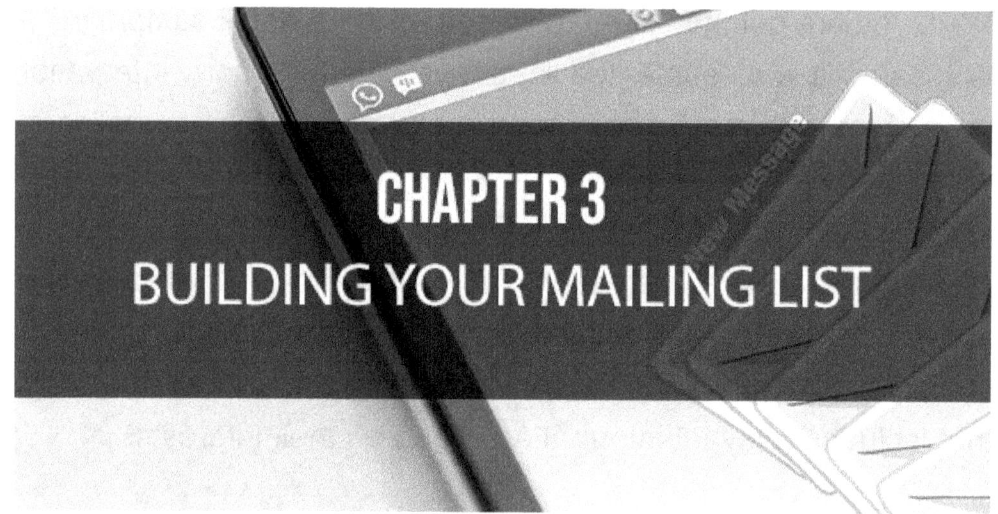

If you want to develop a successful email marketing campaign, you will need to develop a consistent strategy for building and growing your email list. One of the foundational elements of any list-building initiative should be collecting email sign-ups on your website.

People who are interested in your business are probably already visiting your site often. That's why you should be using your website as one of the primary ways to gather email sign-ups.

Lead Magnets

In exchange for signing up for your email list, you need to offer your subscribers something of value. This can be a resource list, a discount coupon, or a free report. In the world of email marketing, this is known as a lead magnet.

Many website visitors are hesitant to enter their email address into an opt-in form on a website because of the perceived risk of receiving more unwanted spam email. However, if you develop a compelling and valuable offer so that potential subscribers will desire your lead magnet enough to outweigh any possible fear of receiving more unwanted email.

> ***Your subscribers know that their email address is valuable to you, and you need to offer them something of equal value in return.***

A good lead magnet will help your website visitors learn a specific skill, accomplish a particular task, or solve a specific problem. The lead magnet on any given page of your website should be directly related to the content on that page.

While you may be required to create multiple lead magnets for different parts of your site over time, the additional work will be well worth it when you significantly improve your opt-in rates. You can save your time and use high-quality PLR content that is relevant for your niche. You can find editable lead magnets on PLR membership sites such as indigitalworks.com.

Here are a few common varieties of lead magnets that you can include to help build and grow your email list.

Free Report or Guide

These are the most common kinds of lead magnet that are used to gain new email subscribers. The report or guide that you offer should help your audience learn about something they are interested in or help them accomplish a specific goal.

For example, if you had a website about marketing, you might offer a free guide that helps your audience create their first Facebook ad campaign. The content of your free report should not otherwise be available on your website.

Resource List

A resource list is merely a list of products, services, tools, and worksheets that will help your subscribers get started more quickly with what you want to teach them. If you have a personal finance blog, you might provide new subscribers with a list of software budgeting tools and resources to help them keep track of their debt, ensure they have the right kinds of insurance, and determine whether they are saving enough for retirement.

Free Trial

If you run a software-as-a-service (SaaS) company, you might think about offering new subscribers a 14- or 30-day trial of your service as a lead magnet. Offering a free trial will get users engaged in your SaaS application and give you the opportunity to send them marketing content via email.

Downloadable Software

If your company produces any kind of software that can be downloaded, you might think about requiring users to enter their email address in order to download the software.

Discounts or Free Shipping

Often, e-Commerce stores will offer a one-time coupon for use on their first order with your company. While providing a discount to new customers might lower the total price of a customer's first order, it will significantly increase the probability that they will become a customer in the first place, because they will be receiving an email about your company's products and services.

Physical Products

If having a physical mailing address for your subscribers is essential, then you can offer an inexpensive-to-produce physical product as your lead magnet. Small tools like flashlights, screwdrivers, and knives are often used as physical product lead magnets. In order to make up the cost of producing and mailing a physical product, you can also charge a small shipping and handling fee that will generally pay for both the product and the shipping.

If you aren't sure what lead magnet will work best for your website, there are a large number of resources that are available online that offer specific ideas for lead magnets. You can do a Google search for "lead magnet ideas" that will return dozens of pages of articles that contain ideas for lead magnets that you can model. You can also check out your competitor's websites to see what kinds of lead magnets they may be offering.

Messaging and Copy

After you've determined the lead magnet that you are going to use, you will need to identify the kind of message you are going to use to get your potential subscribers to sign up for your mailing list.

The language that you use on your opt-in forms will have a significant impact on the number of email signups you receive. By creating a compelling and relevant offer, and using strong language with clear calls-to-action, your opt-in rates will be much higher.

While other list-building strategies might require an upfront cash investment, subscribers that opt-in through your website are effectively free. If you spend sufficient time writing compelling copy, creating a highly-desirable lead magnet, and implementing an opt-in form plugin, your mailing list will steadily grow over time.

Chapter 4 – Writing Emails That Will Inspire Your Audience to Take Action

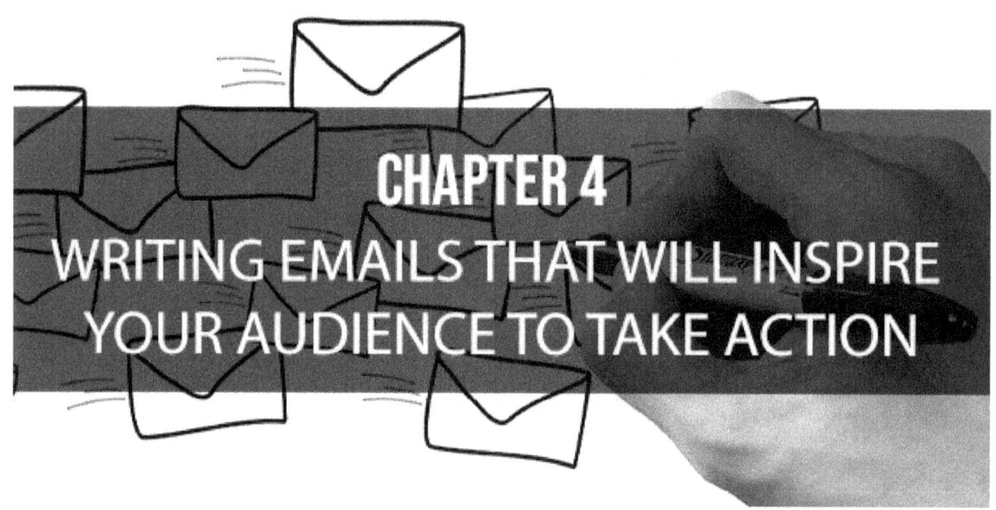

Undoubtedly, you've written thousands of emails in your life. You probably regularly send and receive emails from your family, friends, coworkers, and even strangers on a regular basis. While writing an email to any one person is a straightforward proposition, sending an email to a large group of people requires an entirely different set of skills.

You need to be able to craft a message that not only attracts the attention of a diverse audience, but also clearly communicates a single object and inspires the readers to take the desired action, and it all must be done without the use of audio, video, images, and other dynamic content. You also have to figure out how to deal with the technical peculiarities of email, avoid spam filters, and maintain compliance with anti-spam laws. Writing effective emails is both a science and an art.

Understanding Your Audience

You have to understand who your audience is if you want to write to them effectively. You need to know how old your typical subscribers are, what they do for a living, their gender if they are married, and a ton of other demographics. If you don't know these things, then you should conduct a survey and ask people to share their information with you so that you have a better idea of who makes up your email list.

It is highly recommended that you create a fictional character that epitomizes your typical customer. This is known as an avatar. By creating an avatar, you will have a better idea of who you are marketing to, and it will allow you to get inside the minds of your subscribers.

When you write an email to your mailing list, write as if you are sending a personal message to your avatar. Ask yourself what your avatar would like to hear in order to take action based on your email.

When you write to your avatar and use a lot of "you" language, your subscribers will subconsciously think that you email was explicitly written to them and they will be more likely to engage with the message. You need to keep the focus on your subscribers as much as possible, making sure to make your emails about them, and not about you.

Parts of an Email

When you are getting ready to put together an email, it is easy to think that the only thing that you have to worry about is writing the message body. However, there are several different components of every message that you send to your list.

If you want your email marketing campaign to be successful, then you need to put as much thought and effort into the other parts of your email as you do the main message body. Here are the components of an email that are key.

Subject Line

This is the subject of your message. It is the first thing that your subscribers will see, and it is what will determine whether or not they open your message.

Preheader

The preheader is the preview text that is included after the subject line in some email services like Gmail. It can serve as a second subject line that should further encourage the reader to open your email. If you don't intentionally add a preheader, most email services will use the first sentence or two of your email as a preheader.

"From" Name

This is the name of the person who is sending the email. You want to use your personal name rather than the name of your company because most email users are more likely to open an email from an actual person.

Message Body

This is the main text of your email. It will contain the message that you want to convey to your subscribers.

Call-to-Action

This will be a hyperlink situated at the bottom of your message body that will persuade readers to take a specific action, such as clicking on the hyperlink.

Signature

You want to keep your email signature simple. Long email signatures can be a distraction to the main content of your email.

The best signature is your personal name on the first line and the name of your company on the following line.

Postscript

You may want to consider periodically using a "P.S." below your email signature to serve as a secondary sales tool after your primary email.

Footer

The footer will typically contain an unsubscribe link and other information that you need to include to stay compliant with antispam laws. This might include your mailing address and the name of your company. The footer will likely be the same for every email that you send out.

Keeping Your Emails Balanced

While you will send your audience emails for a variety of reasons, you need to maintain a healthy balance between sending emails that provide value to your audience and email that take value away.

Emails that contain information that is helpful to your audience, at no cost to them, such as educational content, tips, resources, and training videos, provide value to your audience. Emails that ask your audience to purchase a product or take action that benefits you more than them will take value from your audience.

You should consider sending at least two value-added emails to your audience, for every one email that takes it from them. Ideally, you will provide so much value to your audience that they respond to your sales and marketing emails out of sheer gratitude for the value you have already provided.

Writing Great Subject Lines

The most important words that you will write as part of your email marketing strategy is your subject lines. If you write a subject line that is uninspired and doesn't grab the attention of your subscribers, they probably won't open your message.

According to a recent report, 64 percent of people say that they will choose to open an email because of the subject line. If you write a compelling subject line, you are guaranteed to receive higher open rates, which will lead to more click-throughs and more sales.

A well-written subject line can often receive double the open rates of a poorly-written one, which will, in turn, double your clickthrough rates and double the sales generated by the email.

There are also a number of techniques that you can use to modify subject lines to emphasize words and to make unsaid promises about the content of your message.

If you are going to use any of these various techniques, it is essential that you switch them up from email to email and don't use any one of the methods more than twice each month. Subscribers will notice these patterns if you use them too often and will render them ineffective.

Best Practices to Follow with Your Email

When you are creating an email, there are several best practices that you should follow in order to obtain the best results.

Don't Rely on Images

Approximately 10-30 percent of your readers will never click "enable images" on your emails. This means that you should never rely on images to convey critical points in your copy. If you do decide to use pictures, make sure that you use clear and descriptive ALT text. You can use CSS styling to make your ALT text larger and more visible to subscribers that don't enable images.

Avoid Grammar and Spelling Errors

A huge turn off for many email subscribers is poor grammar, capitalization, and spelling errors. If you want to speak with expert authority to your audience, then you need to do so with clear and proper writing.

No one will believe you are an authority on anything if you can't write a complete, grammar and spelling free sentence. Make sure you double-check every email you write for errors or consider having someone else check your email before you send it out.

Include Multiple Hyperlinks

If you have a specific link that you want your readers to click on, then you need to add a total of three hyperlinks to every email. Be sure to hyperlink your main call-to-action at the bottom of your message, as well as just above your email signature.

You also want to add hyperlinks to a few relevant words in the first paragraph of your email to direct readers to the page on your site that you want them to visit. Finally, you need to include a second call-to-action below your email signature and in any postscript that you add in the emails.

Avoid Design-Heavy Emails

Subscribers are more likely to read emails that come from a person rather than a faceless company. While companies frequently use templates in their email, people rarely do. You want to try to avoid using design-heavy templates so that your emails appear more personal.

Only Use One Call-to-Action Per Email

You don't want to try to get your subscribers to do multiple things in any single email. Each email that you send out to your list should have a sole purpose and a single call-to-action that you want them to take. Readers will be less likely to respond if they have to consider which, if any, of your calls-to-action they wish to take.

Have a Clear Unsubscribe Link

Don't try to high or obscure your unsubscribe link. Have a clear unsubscribe link in an average font size. If you decide to obscure your unsubscribe link, your subscribers may report your message as spam, which puts you in jeopardy with your email service provider if your account receives too many spam complaints.

Copywriting is a skill that will take some time to master. For the first several months, the emails that you send won't be perfect, and that's okay. Over time your copywriting skills will improve, and you'll eventually become a great copywriter whose emails get results.

Chapter 5 – Measuring Results and Optimizing Your Strategy

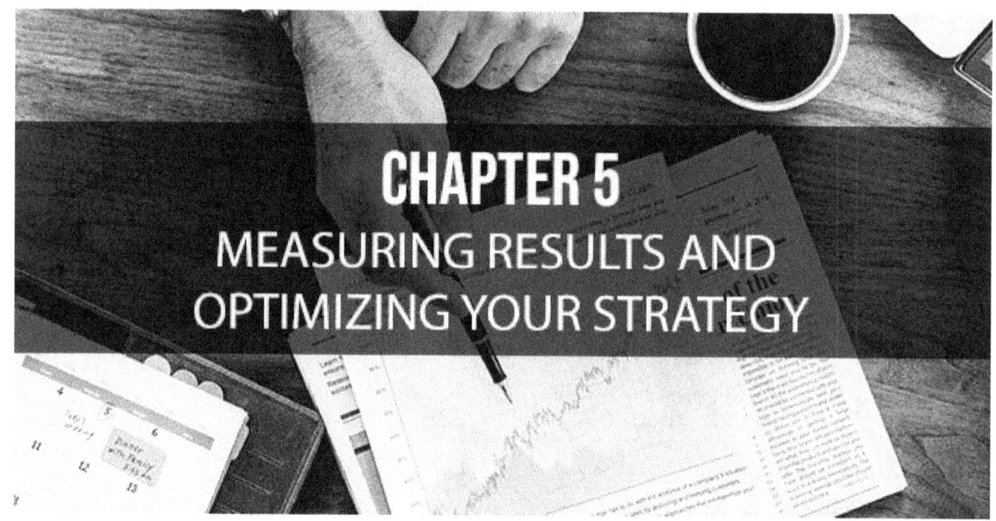

In order to determine whether or not your email marketing campaigns are working, you need to analyze the data from your campaigns. The marketing measures, when all is said and done, always serve to achieve a pre-defined goal, and whether or not you've achieved that goal can only be determined by using the proper KPIs (key performance indicators).

The results that you obtain can also help you to decide whether you can expand your budget for your email marketing strategy.

Also, data analysis is an essential part of being able to optimize your email marketing campaign continually. The only way that you'll be able to gauge the success of your email marketing campaign at all is if you examine and analyze the most critical measurements on a regular basis.

Delivery Rate and Bounce Rates

Among other measurements, email marketing tools will measure the delivery rate, as well as the bounce rate of your emails. These two measurements are mutually complementary and depend on various factors such as technical conditions and sender reputation.

The bounce rate of your emails should always be less than one percent if you want to have a successful campaign. If your bounce rates are higher than this, then you'll need to do some maintenance on your list, and determine which email addresses are no longer valid and remove them from the email list.

Open Rate

The refers to the percentage of subscribers who open the emails you send to them. This figure can be based either on the total number of emails opened, or the number of recipients who opened the email. The latter number is more meaningful and is known as a "unique open rate."

Click Rate

The click rate represents the ratio between the recipients who click on at least one link in an email and the number of emails sent out. You can use this measurement to determine whether your email copy and call-to-actions are compelling enough to get users to take action. This is the most crucial measurement for you to keep track of in your email marketing campaign.

Click-to-Open Rate

This measurement is the ratio of the number of unique clicks to the number of unique opens. The reference value, in this case, is not based on the total number of recipients, but rather the number of recipients who opened the email.

If your click-to-open rates (CTOR) are low, it could mean that the content of the email isn't fulfilling the expectations raised by its subject line. This means that a large number of your subscribers opened the email, but found the content of the email to be uninteresting and didn't click on any of the links.

Conversion Rate

The conversion rate is the percentage of recipients that executed the desired action at the end of the process. This could be anything from purchasing a product, downloading an e-book, or registering for a webinar. You can use this measurement to determine the final success of your email marketing campaign.

Unsubscribe Rate

It is quite reasonable with email subscribers to unsubscribe to an email list because they don't want to get news from the company anymore. The unsubscribe rate describes the ratio of unsubscribes to the total number of emails delivered.

You can typically expect to have an unsubscribe rate of about 0.25 to 0.50 percent for each mailing. As stated previously, it is essential that you include a clearly visible unsubscribe link in every email and to implement an unsubscribe process that is clean and simple.

Email List Growth Rate

The email list growth rate indicates the net increase in the number of email subscribers within a given period. This value is accordingly negative in cases when a mailing list shrinks.

Spam Complaint Rate

This measurement shows how many delivered emails were marked as spam. Your spam complaint rate shouldn't go higher than 0.3 percent. Anything higher than that and you can expect email providers to institute penalties when you try to deliver future emails.

Return on Investment

Your return on investment (ROI), is the financial ratio that is used to measure the return of an entrepreneurial strategy. This measurement compares the profit to the invested capital. When used in email marketing, the term refers to the ratio of the costs required for an email marketing measure to the revenue generated by it.

Defining Your Goals

Before you send out your first emails and start analyzing the results, you need to determine the goals of your email marketing and what you are going to measure. You can set goals like gaining new customers, increasing revenue, or raising brand awareness, or it can be a combination of goals. In order for you to define concrete goals, you are also going to need to establish the appropriate KPIs.

Measurements like click rate, conversion rate, and email list growth rate should always be on your list of metrics to analyze. However, you also need to specify and track the correct KPIs depending on the goals you want to accomplish. For example, if your goal is to gain more subscribers, then you need to focus on the email growth rate, as well as the subscribe/unsubscribe rates. If your number one goal is to increase revenue, then you need to focus on conversion rate.

Continuous Optimization

Analyzing the data associated with your email marketing campaigns is a never-ending process. They should be used to uncover potential areas for improvement in your email marketing campaigns and should immediately flow into planning for your subsequent campaigns.

You will need to compare the measurement results that are achieved by your different email campaigns to get a better sense of what did and didn't work.

As you optimize your email marketing campaign, try different subject lines, sending the emails at different times, placing different call-to-action buttons, and so on, until you find a formula that works. If you discover that specific measurements results aren't satisfactory, then you need to do some digging to find out the cause so you can further optimize your emails to obtain the desired results.

Conclusion

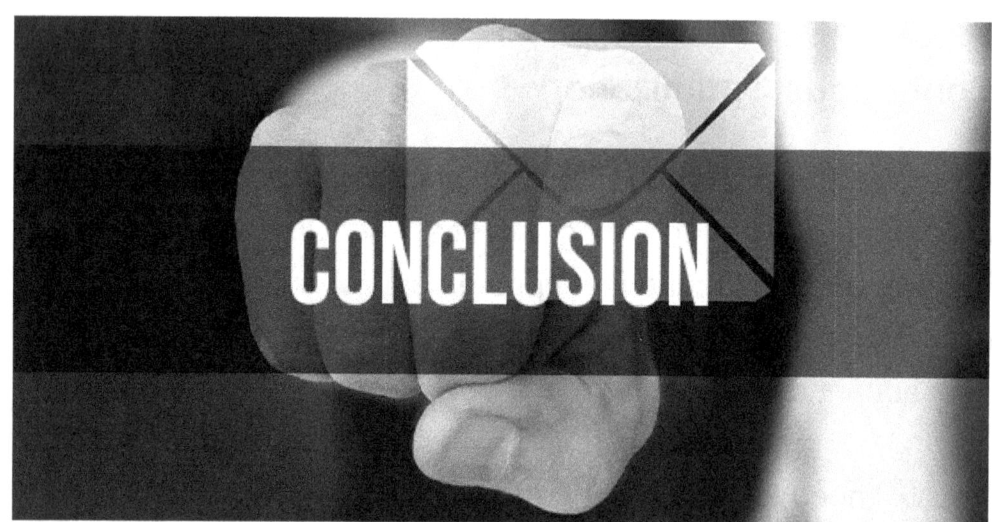

When you are getting started with email marketing, you have to pay special attention to your audience. Since each of your subscribers will have different needs and interests, it is essential that you analyze your data and effectively create a variety of different strategies that you can implement to influence your audience to purchase what you have to offer.

Make sure that you are providing your readers with exciting, dynamic and relevant content to keep your audience happy to receive your messages.

Remember email marketing is an ongoing process to try not to get too frustrated if you don't see immediate results. Your subscribers are knowledgeable, and you will have to work hard to provide them with valuable information and make the connection before you can influence them to make a purchase.

If you make the commitment to implement great business practices, and the more you deliver on your promises, the more your subscribers will trust you, this is the best time to implement email marketing into your overall marketing strategy because information is readily available, and you have many ways to obtain new subscribers and further promote your business.

Taking the time to implement the strategies in this book will help you become a notable email marketer.

Articles

Here are some short articles given as "food-for-thought".

Top 5 Email Marketing Tips For Creating a Successful Campaign

Despite what may have heard, email marketing is a complex process with many moving parts. Despite the complicated nature of this marketing method, you can still have a successful marketing campaign while keeping the process relatively simple. Here are five of the top email marketing tips for creating a successful campaign.

Tip #1 – Make Sure Each Email Contains Obvious Links

The entire purpose of your email marketing is to drive more traffic to your landing page, website, or a product page. Without driving more clicks to your website or page, you won't be able to convert customers. The way you accomplish this is by including a lot of links in the copy of the email and making sure that they can't be missed.

Tip #2 – Make it Easy to Unsubscribe

While this may seem counter-intuitive to make it easier for users to leave your email list, the other option is a lot less appealing. If your users become frustrated when trying to remove themselves from your list, they will eventually start flagging your email as spam. Every time a user marks your email as spam, it counts against your sender reputation with the email providers, which makes it much harder for your emails to end up in the inbox instead of the junk folder.

Tip #3 – Keep Your Text Short and Easy to Scan

Most of the people who get your emails aren't going to read the entirety of your email. They will scan it for the key points that they are interested in. Use bold font and additional colors to highlight keywords or phrases and keep your text short. Having too much text will quickly get your emails deleted and can create more risk of your emails triggering the spam filters.

Tip #4 – Send Test Emails Before You Send to Your Main List

There is nothing worse than sending out an email and then finding out that something broke in the email providers preview pain. Before you send out emails to your entire list, make sure to send a test version to a test account using all of the big email providers. This way you can catch any errors and fix them before you send out to your main list.

Tip #5 – Always Ask User to Add Your Email to Their Contact List

You need to remind users, at every opportunity, that if they want to be sure to continue to get the valuable information they love getting from you that they need to add your email address to their contact list. This way you can ensure that your emails won't automatically be delivered to their junk mail folders.

These top five email marketing tips won't make you a perfect email marketer, but they will put you ahead of your competition. Just utilize these tips as a checklist when you're putting together your email campaigns to ensure it's successful.

The Most Important KPIs for Measuring Your Email Marketing Success

If you're using email marketing campaigns in your business to engage your customers and boost sales, how do you know if they are effective? The only way to know for sure if your email marketing campaign is working is by measuring your key performance indicators (KPIs), which are specific marketing metrics that you can monitor to measure the progress of your email marketing campaigns. Here are the most important metrics to keep in mind for your email marketing campaign.

Deliverability Rate

The deliverability rate refers to where your email messages end up after they've been delivered. It tells you whether your emails ended up in the subscriber's inbox or if they ended up in their spam folder.

Open Rate

This is the percentage of subscribers who opened your email, viewed your email, and whether they opened it more than once. For example, if you send an email to 100 people and 25 of those people opened your email, then your open rate will be 25 percent.

Click-Through Rate

The click-through rate shows you the number of people who clicked on at least one of the links in your email. This is a good way for you to gauge the interest of your subscribers because it shows you how many are taking time to click and dig a bit more.

Conversion Rate

The conversion rate metric allows you to take things a bit further by taking a look at the definite action that you want the clicks to result in. It measures the percentage of people who clicked on a link in your email and completed the desired action, like making a purchase or filling out a form.

Bounce Rate

This metric looks at the number of emails that didn't reach your customers' inbox. There are two different kinds of bounce rates that you should be tracking, the soft bounce rate and the hard bounce rate. The soft bounce rate is when the subscriber's email box is full, or there is a problem with the server. A hard bounce is when there is an invalid email address and your email bounces back.

Unsubscribe Rate

This is the percentage of people who unsubscribe from your email list. If you have a particular email that results in high unsubscribe rates, then you'll want to rethink a few things and adjust your next campaign accordingly.

List Growth Rate

This shows you how quickly your email list is growing. The metric takes into account the bounces, unsubscribes, and the number of contacts that are added to your list during a specific time.

Keeping an eye on these key metrics will help you develop a successful email marketing campaign.

The 5 Best Email Marketing Services for Your Small Business

Choosing the right service for your email marketing can have a significant impact on whether your campaign is successful or not. Email marketing has become one of the most cost-effective tools that a business can include in their overall marketing strategy. The success or failure of an email marketing campaign depends a lot on the software that you choose because it is responsible for making sure that your emails are delivered accurately. If you have decided to make email marketing a priority for your business this year, here are five of the best email marketing services for your small business.

Constant Contact

One of the largest and fastest growing services in the world, Constant Contact is one of the most accessible services for beginning email marketers. It allows you to efficiently manage your email lists, email templates, contacts, marketing calendar and more. Each account you set up provides you with access to easy tracking and reporting, a free image library, social media sharing tools, list segmentation, and a powerful eCommerce integration for Shopify stores.

Drip

Drip is an incredibly powerful email marketing service for bloggers, eCommerce stores, and marketers. They provide a wide range of tools that make it easy to automate your campaign and personalize emails. The service offers users a seamless integration for all popular website builders, which allows you to add sign up forms to your website so you can capture more leads.

SendinBlue

This is a complete SMS and email marketing service for businesses. The platform is incredibly easy to use and provides excellent tools for creating beautiful and highly engaging email campaigns. SendinBlue includes helpful automation tools for beginners that allow you to create workflows, send transactional emails, and segment users.

ConvertKit

ConvertKit is a robust service for authors, bloggers, and marketers, and is incredibly easy to use and extremely powerful. ConvertKit allows you to offer content upgrades and incentives with easy to use email signup forms and comes with an easy to manage auto-responder feature that will enable you to send out drip emails. It lets you segment contact that will help you increase conversions with personalized automated emails.

AWeber

One of the oldest email marketing platforms, AWeber continues to be a popular service provider for small businesses. They offer a broad range of tools for small and medium-sized businesses to manage their email marketing campaigns. It's easy to get started with AWeber as it connects seamlessly to most site building platforms. When you sign up for the service, you get access to ready to use templates, list management, email tracking, and autoresponders.

While there are dozens of email marketing services that you can use, it is essential that you choose the right one for your business. These five choices are great for those who are just getting started building an email marketing campaign.

Quick Tips for Creating Email Copy that Converts

When it comes to your email marketing campaign, the copy is one of the top determining factors on whether your campaign succeeds or fails. Email has become a vital component of online marketing for any business. If you are looking to increase opens, clicks, and conversions with your email marketing campaigns, here are some quick tips for creating copy that converts.

Keep it Simple

You have mere seconds to capture the attention of your audiences, so you want to make sure that you use simple copy in all your emails, as well as on your landing pages. Don't use complicated words or industry jargon in your text; instead; you want to write as if you are speaking to a friend.

Make it Scannable

The last thing you want to do is overwhelm your reader with long paragraphs and tons of copy. Create a design for your emails that break up your text into shorter sections with punchy subheads and numbered or bulleted lists. This will allow the reader to quickly read through the email and grasp the message you are trying to get across.

Talk About Benefits Instead of Features

You want to write compelling copy that lets the reader know what's in it for them. You can do this by talking about how your product or service will benefit them rather than merely listing all the features.

Use More "You" and Less "We"

You always want to keep the focus of your copy on your readers, rather than providing unnecessary information about you or your company. Those who have subscribed to your emails are looking for how your products are going to meet their needs and how they can help them. You can do this by being more customer-centric and using the word "you" more in your email copy.

Align the Copy with the Subject Line

If you can get your subscribers to open your emails, then you need to make sure you deliver on what you promised in the subject line. If you don't, you will more than likely lose their trust. You have to make sure that the copy of your email is in line with the subject line, as well as the preheader.

Use SEO Keywords Judiciously

It is always important to use keywords in your email copy that will boost your readers' interest as well as increase your chances of success with search engines. However, you need to make sure your content is useful and well-written, and you have to avoid trying to fit in too many keywords that don't belong.

If you want to increase the success of your email marketing campaigns, then you have to create copy that converts. These six quick tips can help you create the kind of text for your email campaigns that successfully convert more customers.

Important Things You Need to Know to Run a Successful Email Marketing Campaign

Did you know that there are around 269 billion emails sent out every day? That's a lot of competition for you to try and gain your audience's attention. That's why it's critical for you to learn how to run an email marketing campaign the right way, so you can reach your audience and keep their interest. Here are some of the most important things that you need to know to run a successful email marketing campaign.

Know Your Goals

All good marketing strategies start with setting goals, and email marketing is no different. To run a successful email marketing campaign, you need to think about what it is you want to achieve. Here are some typical goals for an email marketing campaign.

- Welcoming new subscribers
- Boosting engagement
- Nurturing existing subscribers
- Re-engaging subscribers
- Segmenting your subscribers

You can create your email marketing goals according to your overall conversion goals.

Understanding the Different Email Types

Along with knowing your goals, you also have to understand the different types of emails that you can send out. While people group these in different ways, here are the three critical types of emails.

- Promotional emails – these emails talk about sales and offers and are self-promotional.
- Relational emails – these give subscribers what you've promised them, like a gift, weekly newsletter, or relevant information that they can use.
- Transactional emails – these include subscriber signup confirmations, welcome messages, order or purchase confirmations
- Acknowledgments of changes to subscriber information and are usually triggered by a subscriber's actions.

Know Your Audience

If you're just getting started with email marketing, then you're going to have to make some educated guesses if you want to target your content. After you send out your first campaign, you'll start to be able to collect subscriber information so you'll have better data to work with for your next campaign. You can gather data from Google Analytics or Facebook Insights to get demographics, interests, locations, and other pertinent information to give you a better snapshot of your audience.

Use the Right Technology

The best email marketing services that you can use will have tools that will help you create more successful email marketing campaigns. Some of the features that you want to look for are, easy campaign creation and automation, integrations with software you already use, ways to segment your audience, and in-depth analytics on the performance of your email campaigns.

Understanding these four essential aspects of email marketing will help you get started on the right track to creating a successful marketing campaign for your business.

How to Get More Email Subscribers with Social Media

It can be a daunting task to grow your list of email subscribers; however, if your business is active on social media, you have a tremendous tool at your disposal. Social media can get you in front of a broader audience, which will allow you to gain more subscribers. Here are several easy ways to get more email subscribers with social media.

Use a Simple Sign-Up Form

No matter what size business you have, you need to make signing up for your email list easy. If you are using Facebook, dedicate a tab at the top right-hand side of your page for an email form. This way people just have to click on the icon to visit your sign-up form. There are several different options to add and set up an email sign-up form to your Facebook business profile.

Preview Premium Content on Your Social Profiles

If your business creates premium content, you can offer potential subscribers that content for free when they sign up for your email address. If you have white papers, eBooks, infographics or other premium content to give away, set up a landing page for each one to generate new subscribers from that content. Post, tweet and share excerpts from the content to drive interest and traffic.

Share an Incentive for Sign Ups

Incentives can help when it comes to increasing the number of new subscribers to your email list. Many times users just need a little push to take action and subscriber. Advertising the incentive on social media will draw even further attention for your offer and get more people to sign up. Make sure that you include a picture and a strong call-to-action when you post about these incentives.

Host Webinars to Gain Subscribers

An easy way to share the human side of your company is by hosting a webinar about your business. You can present your business by having someone from your company to discuss a relevant topic with your target audience. One of the main goals of hosting a webinar is to capture leads in the form of new subscribers. You can use your social media platforms to advertise and share the link to your webinar.

Hold a Giveaway, Contest, or Sweepstakes

One of the most effective ways to increase your email list is by using your social media platforms to host sweepstakes, contests, and giveaways. While many marketers hold games to grow their following on the various social media platforms, the primary goal should always be to build your subscriber list.

Continuing to grow your subscriber list is a vital part of the success of your business. These tips will help you reach people who already follow you on social media to increase new subscribers.

Best Ways to Improve Your Email Marketing Open Rates

While many people may think that email marketing is dead, it still has one of the highest engagement rates of any marketing strategy. Plus, with an average return of $44.25 for every $1 spent, email marketing also has one of the highest returns on investment. The key to taking advantage of this is to find a way to stand out from the crowd. One easy way to figure out if your efforts are paying off is to pay attention to the open rates of your email campaigns. Here are some of the best ways that you can improve the open rates for your email marketing campaigns.

Create an Engaging Subject Line

The first thing that consumers see on any emails is the subject line. If you haven't tested and optimized yours, then you are leaving money on the table. A/B testing isn't just for your landing pages and websites; it is also an essential part of your email marketing. You want to aim for creating a casual and personal opening line.

Write Quality Content

If your customers come to expect your business to send engaging, entertaining, and informative emails, you'll see a substantial increase in your open rates. However, if you are sending information that they can find elsewhere, or you send them nothing but promotional emails, your messages will end up in the trash bin. One of the best ways to keep your open rates high is by sending high-quality emails less frequently.

Send at the Right Time

In marketing, timing is everything. This is especially true when it comes to email marketing. You want to make sure that you are sending emails at the best times based on the audience, message, and intent. You can do some testing to find this out, or you can do your research on the industry to determine the typical results.

Avoid Spam Filters

The filters on email servers are becoming more and more sophisticated, and if your emails end up in subscribers' spam folders, you'll see your open rate plummet. If you want to stay out of spam folders, then you need to make sure you avoid sending emails that look like spam. Limit the number of links in your message and make sure it doesn't read like a brochure.

These are some of the best ways to ensure your emails get opened. If you want to run an email marketing campaign that is successful, then you need to work on increasing your open rates.

5 Must-Have Components of an Email Marketing Campaign

Email marketing has always been a powerful marketing channel, and automation makes the entire process lot more effective, faster, and smarter. If you want to continue to see a positive ROI, then your campaign must be done right. If you have seen a decrease in your email marketing campaign performance, then you might be missing one of these five must-have components of an email marketing campaign.

A Plan

You have to have a plan in place before you can even start your email marketing campaign. You need to create a content strategy that includes topics that are relevant to your audience. They should be topics that are based on their interests. To ensure that you keep on schedule, create a content calendar that outlines the release dates for each campaign.

Best Performing Subject Lines

The subject lines that you include in your emails will significantly influence open rates. You want to avoid confusing, generic, misleading, and over-the-top subject lines. Make the subject lines short, informative and to the point for the best results. The subject line should set reader expectations and provide them with the jist of the email. Refrain from using all caps and spammy keywords like "free," "gift," and "bonus."

Personalization

Personalizing your emails is one of the easiest ways to stand out in your subscribers' inboxes. Sending personalized emails will help to build trust in the mind of your audience. A simple personalization trick, like addressing readers by their first name, can prove to be incredibly useful. It has been shown that by personalizing everything from the subject line to the products offered, can help to increase click-through rates, which can lead to a significant increase in revenue.

Segmentation

When it comes to successful marketing strategies, one-size-doesn't-fit all. Email marketing focuses on getting subscribers to take action, and it requires you to have a solid understanding of your recipients. Knowing your audience better can help you create segments that will allow you to tailor content to each subscriber, which will ensure better engagement.

Mobile Optimization

Sending out a non-responsive email will appear outdated on a mobile device and tablets. With more and more people opening their emails on their smartphones and tablets, mobile optimization needs to become a natural part of the process. If you want to run a successful email marketing campaign, make sure you are optimizing your emails for mobile phones and tablets.

If you want to run a successful email marketing campaign, then you need to ensure that these five must-have components are included in every campaign you send out.

5 Mistakes to Avoid in Your Email Marketing Campaign

These days, most businesses have an email marketing strategy. However, with more than 294 billion emails sent every day, it is crucial for your business to stand out from the crowd. The last thing you want to do is spend your time and effort on creating an email campaign only to have your emails go unread. Here are five mistakes to avoid making with your email marketing campaign.

Sending Your Emails from a donotreply@yourdomain.com

Sending your emails from a donotreply or noreply email is incredibly unwelcoming and uninviting. Don't be shocked if your open rate is low is you send your emails from one of these addresses. You always want to make sure you are sending emails from an address that your customers can reply to if they have issues or questions.

Sending Image Only Based Emails

Only about 33 percent of email subscribers will have their images turned on by default. This means that nearly two-thirds of your subscribers will not be able to read your email, but instead be faced with a long, empty box. Plus, text-only emails have a 40 percent higher click-through rate than those that contain only images. If you do decide to use pictures, make sure that you repeat everything in simple text.

Not Linking to Your Website

The entire goal of email marketing is to get people to click through to your company website. Your email needs to include at least one link that sends subscribers to a dedicated landing page that continues the email message. Similar to marketing campaigns that utilize search engines, you want to create a dedicated landing page for your email campaign, making sure that you include the link in the email.

Using a 'One-Size-Fits-All' Approach

The most effective form of any marketing method is relevance. Your message needs to be relevant to your subscribers. The one-size-fits-all approach no longer works. Being relevant shows that you care about your subscribers. Only 11 percent of businesses segment their email lists, which makes creating relevant email marketing campaigns a competitive advantage for your business. Your segmentation can be basic or complex. By segmenting your list and customizing your message, you'll have more engaged customers and higher click-through rates.

Ignoring Mobile

Fifty-four percent of all emails are now opened on a mobile device, and 40 percent of mobile users check their email more than four times a day. If your email campaign isn't optimized for mobile devices many of your subscribers may not be able to read your message.

Avoiding these five mistakes can ensure that your email marketing campaign is successful. Email is still the most preferred communication channel for most customers, so creating an effective email campaign will help you out-perform the competition.

4 Effective Ways to Get More Email Subscribers

One of the most invaluable assets for your business is your email list. However, this is only true if it contains subscribers that are eager to listen to what you have to say and who want to buy your products. According to recent research, the average email open rate is only 32 percent, but with an effective strategy and smart planning, you can grow your list and keep your engagement rates higher. Here are four practical ways that you can get more qualified email subscribers.

Craft a More Compelling Offer

The most important and most significant way to increase your subscribers is to make the offer more appealing. While you can change the colors of your buttons, and improve small factors in your email, if you don't have a proposal that converts, you're wasting your time and money. You need to focus on giving your target audience what they really want if you want to get more subscribers.

Make the Process as Easy as Possible

The simpler you make your opt-in form, the more likely someone will be willing to subscribe. By removing the name field on your form, you'll grow your list faster. Every step that you can take to make your opt-in form simpler will help you increase your subscribers and build your audience. The fewer steps you have between a consumer being interested and them signing up will help your list grow.

Encourage Sharing

If you have an email that you think will get a particularly strong reaction from your subscribers, you can encourage them to forward the email to their family and friends. You will need to make sure that you have a way for new people to sign up and ensure that those who get forwarded the email don't click on the unsubscribe button. As long as you can include details about these two factors in the email, you can ask your current subscribers to forward the email so you can find more like-minded prospects.

Give Users More Control Over the Content

Part of your goal when growing your email list is to make sure that people don't unsubscribe. If you start to notice an increase in unsubscribes, it might be because people are overwhelmed. To combat this issue, you can offer a light subscription or even different leveled plans. The idea is to try and keep subscribers on your list, even if they aren't receiving your entire lineup of emails.

If you want to start generating great results with your email, then you need to put in the time and effort to build a great list. These four strategies are a great way to get more email subscribers.

About the Author

C.X. Cruz was born in Puerto Rico and have lived in the New York City area since he was 14 years old. He holds graduate degrees from the State University of New York and Honolulu University in Computer Science. He has worked for European investment banks such as UBS, and for American banks such as Goldman Sachs. His hobbies include forestry and rowing.

As a very young graduate student, Cruz thought of publishing books. It was extremely difficult to publish a book using the traditional methods 30 years ago. He gave up on this publishing dream back then. Thankfully, there are numerous ways to become a self-publisher today. The internet has democratized many businesses such book publishing. Cruz can bring you great content and a great price. Never stop reading and learning. Cruz knows you will enjoy reading his books!

Legal

No Liability

Under no circumstances will the product creator, programmer or any of the distributors of this product, or any distributors, be liable to any party for any direct, indirect, punitive, special, incidental, or other consequential damages arising directly or indirectly from the use of this product. This product is provided "as is" and without warranties.

Use of this product indicates your acceptance of the "No Liability" policy. If you do not agree with our "No Liability" policy, then you are not permitted to use or distribute this product (if applicable.) Failure to read this notice in its entirety does not void your agreement to this policy should you decide to use this product.

Applicable law may not allow the limitation or exclusion of liability or incidental or consequential damages, so the above limitation or exclusion may not apply to you.   The liability for damages, regardless of the form of the action, shall not exceed the actual fee paid for the product.

InDigitalWorks.com

Copyright

www.ingramcontent.com/pod-product-compliance
Lightning Source LLC
Chambersburg PA
CBHW071948120726
48001CB00005B/2090